Cover to Cover Bible Study

7 Sessions for Homegroup and Personal Use

The Divine Blueprint

God's extraordinary power in ordinary lives

Gary Pritchard

Copyright © CWR 2004

Published 2004 by CWR, Waverley Abbey House, Waverley Lane,
Farnham, Surrey GU9 8EP. Reprinted 2010.

The right of Gary Pritchard to be identified as the author of this work has been
asserted by him in accordance with the Copyright, Designs and Patents Act 1988
Sections 77 and 78.

See back of book for list of National Distributors.

Unless otherwise indicated, all Scripture references are from the Holy Bible:
New International Version (NIV), copyright © 1973, 1978, 1984 by the
International Bible Society.

Concept development, editing, design and production by CWR.
Front cover image: Roger Walker.
Printed in Latvia by Yeomans Press Ltd

ISBN 978-1-85345-292-5

Contents

Introduction

One of my fondest childhood memories is of the annual local community day trip to the nearest beach in South Wales. Much of the fine detail of those much anticipated excursions has now blurred into history, but a few things remain crystal clear. One of my most vivid recollections is of sinking my sockless toes deep into the cool sand of the beach. I'm still not sure why this simple act was such a wonderful experience. But that gritty plunge through the warm powder-white surface down into the cloying damp shingle below remains a very real and sensual recollection. Maybe it was the freedom from the day-to-day restriction of shoes that made it so lovely, or simply the tactile bliss of thousands of grains of sand squeezing through my toes.

Perhaps it was one of the rare unexplainable occasions in life where one feels connected to creation – God's creation. Similar to those mornings when you wake up and everything in the world feels just as it should – an amorphous sense of deep harmony and simple peace.

Our relationship with the Scriptures can be similar. The sometimes over-familiar routine of regularly engaging with God's Word can momentarily be suspended to allow a shaft of revelation light of truth into an area of our lives. This can be especially true when we consider the Old Testament.

Many feel that this considerable portion of Scripture contains useful life stories, interesting historical contexts and maybe some prophetic strands that foreshadow Christ's ministry. I'd like to suggest that the Old Testament in fact contains the blueprint that not only provides the lineage of Christ, but also sets up the worldview and vision that was imagined by the Creator for His creation.

Some would see this blueprint as forming part of the

basis of our personal faith-walk with Jesus and, crucially, mapping out a righteous lifestyle right at the heart of the nitty-gritty details of our day-to-day routines and existence.

Thank the Lord for all the fabulous teaching and God-inspired resources that we have at our fingertips in our modern culture, but could it be that we still have missed something crucial? Well, the answer is yes – in one small but critical way.

A philosopher by the name of Plato has probably had more of an impact on our Christian worldview that almost anyone else – apart from Christ of course. Plato was an aristocratic Greek philosopher born 500 years before Jesus. Because of war he had lost his substantial position of privilege in his culture. He cleverly set out to restore his position of power by introducing a plan so devast-atingly convincing that we still live with its legacy today. He slowly and carefully convinced his fellow Grecians that they had a serious spiritual problem – one that he just happened to have a solution for! He painted a picture of a divided universe. A historian friend describes Plato's strategy like this: you describe a realm that is removed from life and call it perfect, real, ideal, a must-get-there kind of place (heaven if you like). You tell people that where they live and work is not 'real', not ideal, not perfect and definitely not where they should be. And then you tell them that you just happen to have what it takes to get them from where they are to where they should be. Sounds like a classic sales technique doesn't it? This ploy worked so well that they imagined that in order to reach this ideal realm (a spiritual heaven) described by Plato, they would need someone wise to direct them – enter Plato!

Because many of the early Christian church leaders were from a Greek rather than a Hebrew background, they inadvertently introduced Plato's influence into Christian thinking – and it still remains with us today. The impact is to create a division between the heavenly and the earthly – a division that God never intended.

So, for example, a Hebrew life perspective (the one that Jesus grew up in) viewed work, witness, prayer and everyday life as inseparable spheres – all merged together into something they called the walk of faith. Conversely, the Greek (or Platonic) filter has impacted on us by dividing things into the divine and the earthly, the sacred and the secular, the spiritual and the worldly. In other words, the Hebrews had no notion of 'church' business and then everyday life – it was all the same to them.

Most days we all have a situation at work or in the home where an instinctive prayer – audible or otherwise – comes naturally. Yet this simple day-to-day act of 'normal' faith in action is often viewed as having less significance than, say, the official fellowship prayer meeting. This has an influence on how we read the Scriptures (and live our lives) too, so that the great Bible men and women of faith whose lives and acts we admire so much, can be elevated to a status that is beyond us. In truth, these heroes of faith were flesh and blood normal believers with everyday lives (and often doubts) like you and me. In their stories we see God's extraordinary power in ordinary lives.

These study aids will revisit the lives of some of the famous Old Testament characters – but with a difference. We will attempt to peek behind the heroic acts and miraculous deeds and seek to uncover the fragile, normal everyday elements too. Hopefully such a study will inspire us all to see ourselves (yes us!) as potential vessels for God's work – whatever our circumstances.

Otherwise, as the saying goes, we risk becoming so heavenly-minded that we are of no earthly use!

WEEK 1

'A Woman's Place is ... Doing the Will of God'

Opening Icebreaker

Form pairs (with someone you don't know or don't know very well) and introduce yourselves. Get to know each other. After five minutes, you are to introduce each other to the group, saying one thing you have in common with the other person. Try and find something a bit unusual. For example, you both have children under the age of five, or you both excelled in maths at school.

Bible Readings

* Judges 4:1–24
* John 18:1–11

Opening Our Eyes

Have you read certain commentaries on women in the Bible and squirmed at their rather patronising tone? I am sure that they are well intended, but often such reviews airbrush out some of the less, shall we say, 'unladylike' aspects of the biblical accounts. A scan of the story of the only female Judge of Israel, Deborah, frankly requires a strong stomach. She begins with a prophetic command to Hebrew army leader Barak to oversee the slaughter of a great Canaanite army. But the story goes on to be even more bloodthirsty as it describes the downfall of their leader Sisera, who, lulled into a false sense of security in the tent of the woman Jael, was then murdered gruesomely with a tent peg through his temple!

Deborah's prophetic words to Barak and his clear respect for her as a woman of God, make for compelling reading. In fact Barak is so nervous about the action he is prompt-ed to undertake, that this mighty leader of the Israelite army pleads with her, 'If you go with me, I will go ...' (Judg. 4:8).

It helps to remember that the book of Judges speaks of an in-between time in Israel's history. It is easy to identify with such a time even today – the gap between what God promises and when it actually becomes reality. For God's people then it was the time between the Exodus from Egypt and inheriting the promised land.

In our contemporary culture with talk of modern-day revivals and transformation in other parts of the world, for those in the west, for example, it can be a frustrating living, with a sense of an 'in-between time' – the time between the promise and the reality.

It was into just such a sense of confusion that Deborah intervened with stunning effect. Having consented to join

Barak in seizing the moment to rout God's enemy, the Lord threw the army into a panic – no Israelite could take the credit.

The account reminds us of the ambiguous mixture of human and divine in the way God works in history. Like Deborah, we need to hold on to faith in God's miraculous presence and promise, yet recognise that human action is often instrumental in the outcome of events. In other words, there is a mixture of the ordinary and the extra-ordinary – a prophetic word and mysterious circum-stances that throw a trained army into panic, and timid commanders of armies and women who take matters into their own hands.

But the book of Judges would have us see that God is part of it. Deborah interprets and speaks God's word. She instils God's courage. And victory comes through God's action. Israel is saved and has rest for another generation. That was the Hebrew worldview – no division between the heavenly and the 'earthly' – it is a seamless and dynamic relationship between God and His creation.

This is the divine blueprint, one that God set up to ensure that when His people hear His voice and take the human action required – the victory can be won. Our heavenly Father seems to love to work in partnership with His Church – a Church that is imperfect, often confused, and regularly fearful. It is from this unlikely union – divine power and human weakness – that God can perform great acts.

So often we either act in our own strength (without hearing God first), or are frozen by fear of what others may think if we do obey. It is only when we consult the divine blueprint that we can live lives in accordance with the Divine Architect.

Discussion Starters

1. What circumstances would cause you to spiral into feeling fearful?

_____

_____

_____

_____

_____

_____

_____

2. Do you know the symptoms of fear when they surface in your own life? What strategies do you have to counteract such fear?

_____

_____

_____

_____

_____

_____

_____

3. In what ways do you think that contemporary culture has contributed to an almost inevitable sense of disappointment at certain times of our lives?

_____

_____

_____

_____

_____

_____

_____

4. Recall a time when, despite feeling weak in a situation, you sensed God's strength.

_____

_____

_____

_____

_____

_____

_____

5. Many Christians turn to Scripture for comfort in tough moments – what scriptures spring to mind as 'comfort' words or promises?

_____

_____

_____

_____

_____

_____

_____

6. Do you feel that we live in an 'in-between time' like Deborah, and what promises of God do you look forward to seeing realised?

_____

_____

_____

_____

_____

_____

_____

Personal Application

It is a sad fact that we can become cripplingly disillusion-ed or disappointed during our walk of faith. This can be triggered by being let down by a close friend, or maybe a symptom of being overly idealistic and having unreason-able expectations. We have seen that Deborah lived during an 'in-between time in Israel's history', a period that seemed to lack any evidence of God's presence with His people. At such times in our own lives it is crucial that we remember that God is right at our side, even if it doesn't feel like it. Once we establish this in our hearts, we can then remain strong, even in our weakness – full of hope even though the evidence of victory seems lacking.

Seeing Jesus in the Scriptures

As a witness to events leading up to Christ's death, it would have been easy to conclude that things weren't going to plan. He was betrayed, captured, tortured, mocked and finally crucified. To read about this without understanding the divine purpose, would be to have a distorted picture of Jesus and His mission. It was because the Son of God was operating with an intimate trust in His Father that He was able to stay focused even in the most distressing moments of His last days on earth. Such trust (despite seemingly negative circumstances) comes as a result of a deep relationship with God – a trust that can see off the storms of doubt and disappointment when they crash upon the shore of our lives.

WEEK 2

To Love and to Obey

Opening Icebreaker

Use a mock 'torch' (or a real one) as a prop for this activity. All participants sit in a large circle (it works best to sit on the floor but chairs are OK). To get the ball rolling, the facilitator holds the torch and shares some information with the group. This can either be a goal related to the class or a means of sharing some personal information, eg, 'I want to improve my understanding of the Bible.'

Bible Readings

- Jonah 1:1–17; 4:1–11
- Matthew 12:39–41; 16:4
- Luke 11:29–32
- Hebrews 12:25–29

Opening Our Eyes

Most of us are familiar with the story of Jonah and the whale (the Bible says it was a big fish). It is one of the staple Sunday School Bible stories that children love. The emphasis of Jonah's story here, however, is not the dramatic 'whale' narrative, but how God overcame Jonah's considerably flawed character, once again using less than ideal circumstances to get His will done.

You'll remember that God commanded Jonah to go to Nineveh and preach to them about their sinfulness, calling them to repentance. This is the only time in the Old Testament where Israel is commanded to actively pursue the Gentiles. God's covenant with Abraham mentioned that through Abraham's descendants God would bless the nations, but no Israelite was commanded to go to the nations and tell them about God. They were to have a passive witness. The Gentiles were supposed to see the difference between their society and Israel's and be attracted to it. The Old Testament is full of examples of Gentiles who became Jewish proselytes and worshipped Yahweh; for example, Ruth, Jael, Shamgar, the woman at Jericho.

What is Jonah's reaction to God's command? He refuses – he doesn't say anything, he just leaves town. Notice the route he took: he went *down* to Joppa. He found a ship going down to Tarshish, so he went *down* (NKJV) into the boat – perhaps Jonah should have been warned that things were about to go seriously downhill as a consequence of ignoring his Creator!

With Jonah safely on board with his fellow travellers, God then sends a wind, causing the sea to heave. But it is the heathen sailors who start praying (even if they are not sure who to pray to!), while the man of God is complacently sleeping below. Jonah's lack of reaction is significant. Sin hardens the heart and makes us insensitive, and here we see that he is insensitive to what God is doing. We also see the first of many contrasts between the heathens and Jonah. Jonah is insensitive, but the heathens are aware that something out of the ordinary is going on, even though they are praying to false gods.

The heathen sailors even had more compassion than so-called 'chosen' Jonah. They did not want to throw him overboard and tried desperately to get to land without having to do that. They begged Jonah's God's pardon for what they had to do; in contrast to the man of God who had no compassion on the people of Nineveh.

God responded by calming the sea – the sailors then recognised that the true God is Jonah's God, so they prayed to Yahweh. They were probably devotional vows that they would follow and obey God; unlike Jonah who simply disobeyed Him.

If we move to later in the story we see the successful outcome of Jonah's struggles with God, but how much easier it would have been for him to simply obey God in the first place.

Discussion Starters

1. What do you understand to be 'the fear of God'?

_____

_____

_____

_____

_____

_____

2. Do you feel that the general mistrust of authority in our culture has had an impact on how people view and trust God?

_____

_____

_____

_____

_____

_____

3. Discuss examples of simple ways of living an obedient godly lifestyle.

_____

_____

_____

_____

_____

_____

4. Give some examples of how being obedient (in any environment) has proved significant and conversely how being disobedient has proved significant?

_____

_____

_____

_____

_____

_____

5. Do you know of any example where a non-believer has apparently displayed more godly character than, say, some Christian colleague or friend?

_____

_____

_____

_____

_____

_____

6. Have you ever had to deliver some tough news or discipline to someone – how did that feel and what strategy did you use?

_____

_____

_____

_____

_____

_____

7. Have you ever felt that you have let God down so badly that you have become disqualified from serving Him (or do you know someone else who feels that way)?

_____

_____

_____

_____

_____

_____

Personal Application

Most of us have lives that parallel Jonah's experience. God calls us, but we often rebel. We search for life in everything else but God, until we come to a point in our life where we are so low that we finally recognise our helplessness and come to the conclusion that salvation is only from the Lord.

Although Jonah's story seems to highlight the reluctant obedience of a 'spiritually deaf' man, it is also extremely comforting. The divine blueprint, it seems, never rules out God's chosen vessels – even if they are initially as stubborn as Jonah. Those who choose to obey God without a fight are not more 'chosen' of God – but they do avoid so much of the considerable heartache that comes as a result of disobedience.

Seeing Jesus in the Scriptures

It has been said that the Church in our culture doesn't allow saints to feel that they can fail. As a consequence, when certain Christians sense that they have let God down badly, they run from the Church in shame or embarrassment. What a contrast to Christ. He was never slow in calling sin what it was, or revealing suspect motives in His critics, but how often do we see Him embracing the sinner – the woman caught in adultery, for example.

Surely the Church should be the one place where we are allowed to feel that if we do stumble we have fellow believers who will stand with us and support us?

WEEK 3

Fit for a Queen

Opening Icebreaker

Many of us doodle from time to time, to relax or to pass
the time while we are doing something else (like talking
on the telephone). Usually we think of doodles as small
drawings that have no meaning at all, but some experts
think that sometimes they reveal our innermost hopes
and fears. If you were to doodle now while thinking
about this study session, what would the finished doodle
look like?

Bible Readings

- Esther 2:1–18; 8:1–17
- Matthew 6:1–8

Opening Our Eyes

It is fair to say that although we still have a long way to go, our culture allows far more opportunity and equality for women than in past generations. One only has to review the story of Esther to realise a woman's lot in her day. Her time was possibly the lowest point for God's people in Jewish history. They had been scattered and those who remained were ruled over by the powerful King Xerxes.

Frustrated by his rebellious queen, the king dispatched his men to find the most beautiful virgins in the whole empire to replace her, and they were rounded up and brought to Susa.

Once selected, they spent an entire year being prepared – for just one night. The beauty regime they were subjected to makes the cosmetic counter in Harrods look like face painting at a church fete. It went something like this: for six months they were rubbed with oil of myrrh, then for another six months they applied a paste of spices and cosmetics that lightened their skin and removed any blemishes. Their body was then bathed in aromatic perfumes, their eyebrows were plucked, all body hair removed, their hands and feet were painted with henna and then make-up was applied to the face!

At the end of this period, each young woman was brought to spend one night with the king. If she pleased him she could be chosen to be queen. If not, she spent the rest of her days in a harem, which was equivalent to becoming a widow. Most of these young women never saw the king again, but they remained his property and could not leave and could never marry or have relations with another man.

Esther was a beautiful young woman brought up by her

uncle Mordecai. She was one of those singled out for 'trial' for the position of queen. As a Jewess, she was technically forbidden to engage in such a union – but her uncle, for fear of the consequences, tells her to go – with orders *not* to reveal that she is a Jew.

When Esther arrives for 'training' she immediately wins the favour of Hegai, the eunuch in charge of the women. This must have been a harrowing time. It is not the way she would have liked her life to go. She was being prepared to sleep with a man not as a wife but as a 'trialist'. Her life may well be as good as over.

Finally it was her turn, and four years after the beauty contest began, Esther went in to the king. He was im-pressed. He loved Esther more than all the women, we read, and she found favour and kindness with him, so he set the royal crown on her head and made her queen.

Now, depending on your theology, Esther's story throws up an intriguing question that has divided scholars for years. Does God plan and control *all things* from His throne, or does He intervene into our fallen world, using available circumstances and willing vessels to see His will accomplished? In many ways the answer is simply academic – the divine blueprint once again seems to suggest that whatever the means, Father God seeks to join His creation in a partnership to see the miraculous achieved.

Esther found herself up against significant odds and with a trajectory for her life that she hadn't planned or would necessarily have chosen. Yet, in obedience to her fearful uncle and with a pure heart, she made the most of the opportunity that God was able to exploit.

As we will see from the next study this was just the beginning of Esther's story.

Discussion Starters

1. Esther was placed in a position not of her choosing, yet she managed to shine despite the odds. When was the last time you sensed God at work in your life, even when the circumstances seemed out of your control?

_____

_____

_____

_____

_____

_____

2. If you really believe that God is intimately involved in every detail of your everyday life, how does that (or how should that) affect your ambition and behaviour?

_____

_____

_____

_____

_____

_____

3. How much do you feel that your life-path is mapped out in advance? Would sensing God working constantly despite variable circumstances affect how you lived?

_____

_____

_____

_____

_____

_____

4. How much do you think that Esther had to align herself with God's plan? In other words, were the outcomes inevitable, or did she also have to be at her very best to have a chance of finding favour with the king?

_____

_____

_____

_____

_____

_____

_____

5. When was the last time that circumstances that you thought to be negative, turned round to reveal that God's hand was in them all along?

_____

_____

_____

_____

_____

_____

_____

Personal Application

We often idealise other people's circumstances so that we imagine that if only we had their opportunities or life chances, then we'd be able to do God's will. It can become a huge negative force that immobilises and can render us ineffective. If we dare to compare ourselves with those in circumstances that are worse than ours, this can be the beginning of God using us despite the hurdles that stand in our way. By making the most of our given circumstances, like Esther, we can provide the platform for God to add the divine to the human – often with miraculous results.

Seeing Jesus in the Scriptures

It was impossible to pigeonhole Jesus during His ministry – many tried. He was asked trick questions designed to trap Him by taking a certain theological position. He was also courted by certain groups in order to further their own agendas – all without success. Jesus seemed to be able to identify and focus upon the individual motivations and inner motives of people and then cut to the chase. At times He would say 'sell everything and give it to the poor', and at others He applauded extravagant gestures. As such He seemed to be suggesting that a sincere heart was the key to serving God – whatever our circumstances or status in life.

WEEK 4

Standing out from the Crowd

Opening Icebreaker

Tell the group about the 'imaginary friend' you have brought with you. What will your imaginary friend do to help you in this session? For instance, my imaginary friend will poke me every time I start falling asleep – as you can tell, I'm not an evening person.

Bible Readings

- Esther 2:9–18; 8:1–17
- Matthew 16:1–12

Opening Our Eyes

In our last study, we saw how Esther made the most of some alarming circumstances in order to gain a role of significant influence. This was to prove to have more impact than she or anyone could have imagined.

Events were moving fast. Esther's uncle Mordecai was sitting at the king's gate one day, when he overheard two of the king's officials plotting to kill King Xerxes. Mordecai immediately informed Queen Esther of the assassination plan, and Esther told the king. The officials were then intercepted and the plot foiled.

God had raised Esther up to be queen and now He had made the king indebted to Mordecai for his life. Both unlikely events, but such circumstances were to prove critically important for God's people.

King Xerxes meanwhile had promoted one of his nobles, Haman, to a position of high status and power in his kingdom. Haman's family were sworn enemies of the Jewish people, and after clashing with Mordecai Haman persuaded the king to agree to a total destruction of the Hebrews.

Mordecai was distraught. His anguish was that not only were his people about to be killed, but he was the catalyst that had led to this point. He sent word to Esther that their only hope was for her to go in to the king – tell him she was Jewish and beg for his favour.

Mordecai warns Esther, 'Do not think that because you are in the king's house you alone of all the Jews will escape. For if you remain silent at this time, relief and deliverance for the Jews will arise from another place, but you and your father's family will perish. And who knows but that you have come to royal position for such a time as this?' (Esther 4:12–14).

Basically, Mordecai is spelling out clearly to Esther, 'Yes I know that your life is at risk – but this is our only hope, this is your only hope. If you don't do this you will die. Being queen won't save you.' He is giving her two choices – a slim chance, and no chance.

And then he offers this ray of hope: 'Perhaps you becoming queen was all directed toward this one act to save your people.'

King Xerxes during this time, while reviewing recent events, had realised that Mordecai had not been rewarded for the information that had averted his assassination. By the time Esther petitioned the king, he was already planning to honour her uncle. When he discovered that his royal aide Haman had acted from a personal vendetta against Mordecai and was planning the annihilation of the Jews, he became furious. Haman paid with his life.

But it didn't finish there. Mordecai replaced Haman as prime minister. So instead of being annihilated, the Jews now occupied the positions of prime minister and queen over the Persian Empire!

In bold headlines, Esther's story can sound like just another of the great miracle testimonies of the Old Testament. It is only when we read between the lines that we see God once again working out His plan – using flawed individuals to act as vessels to achieve His will, and showing again the relationship between His divine sovereignty and human responsibility.

Esther and her uncle Mordecai had dared to trust God despite all their insecurities, and what a venture it proved to be.

Discussion Starters

1. If we didn't have all the details, Queen Esther could be seen as a highly ambitious achiever. Do you think we judge our public figures fairly?

_____

_____

_____

_____

_____

_____

_____

2. Have you ever gone from being an employee to a boss – what challenges did that throw up?

_____

_____

_____

_____

_____

_____

_____

3. Do you know anyone who has had to show courage in speaking up or honestly confessing something that has jeopardised his or her career or reputation?

_____

_____

_____

_____

_____

_____

_____

4. 'Honesty is the best policy' is now viewed as an old fashioned motto. How realistic do you think it is to live today with such a philosophy?

_____

_____

_____

_____

_____

_____

_____

5. Without having what we could term a 'public faith', Princess Diana was seen as a role model to many people. Why do you think she had such an impact on our society?

_____

_____

_____

_____

_____

_____

_____

6. How do you feel a woman's role in society has changed from your grandparents' generation?

_____

_____

_____

_____

_____

_____

_____

Personal Application

God uses a different measure to most people when gauging the value or status of an individual. It is only as we are seduced by the values of society that we begin to sense conflict in our lives. Standing up for what we believe or living with integrity when the pressure is to follow the crowd, ensures that we live by God's values and not those of the media or contemporary culture.

Seeing Jesus in the Scriptures

An old but still powerful saying suggests that faith is spelt RISK. Jesus had to take some serious risks during His lifetime. He risked His reputation when challenging the religious rulers, He risked being let down by choosing flawed individuals as His disciples, and He literally risked and gave His life in order to fulfil His mission. Many of us lead non-risky lives compared to others around the world in unstable environments and war zones. Jesus should inspire us to take at least one risk – to trust Him and live lives that honour and exalt Him.

WEEK 5

Stumbling Block or Stepping Stone?

Opening Icebreaker

Most children look forward to change – they are fascinated by how a butterfly emerges from a chrysalis; how roses placed in a vase slowly bend their heads, their petals becoming dry tissue; that clouds are shape shifters, holding hidden messages in their uncertain depths. Tell the group how you reacted to change as a child. And how you tend to react to it now.

Bible Readings

• Daniel 1:1–21

Opening Our Eyes

We have seen as we read of people who have tapped into the divine blueprint, that one of the recurring themes is their often less than favourable circumstances. This time it's Daniel.

Yet again we have one of God's children thrust into a situation not of his choosing. Daniel is taken captive as a youth and sent against his will to a foreign land, with strange customs and unfamiliar food. During many of the lonely, cold nights, Daniel must have questioned God's participation in his life. He probably would never see his parents again, his prospects were decidedly limited and he even had to endure a change of name given by his new masters.

Most Bible studies of Daniel quickly cut to the exciting developments of his life, but it is useful to pause for a moment at this particular stage of his formative years.

How many times have you heard fellow believers des-cribe their troublesome circumstances as the cause of their limited effectiveness for God? Difficult family issues, an unreasonable boss, financial constraint, uninspiring worship at the church meeting and so on. Maybe some or several of these circumstances are real issues for you right now and it would be foolish to suggest that genuinely difficult situations should be ignored or dismissed as trivial. Even if you are blessed to be free of such problems, we all know someone who is battling with some tough issue in their lives.

The key question here, however, is not how we 'feel' at such a time – more how we choose to respond. Daniel had every right to feel aggrieved with his life circumstances – abandoned by parents, by God even?

He made a key choice however – a choice of whether to be a victim or an overcomer.

The great Martin Luther King had a straight talking reality check for his fellow black Americans during the famous race struggles in the US. He said that if they saw themselves as victims, then they would always remain victims. He challenged them to rise up from their considerably disadvantaged circumstances and strive for excellence wherever they could.

Daniel had the same attitude – either he could lie down and submit to his circumstances or he could believe that God was indeed God and keep Him at the centre of his life, seeking to connect the divine call with human desire. Simply put, he made a choice to trust God.

Daniel came into the category of 'ready and willing' to do God's work – despite what were seemingly limited opportunities. If we can dare to do likewise, then who knows how the divine blueprint can be implemented in our own everyday extraordinary lives?

Discussion Starters

1. How do you think you would feel if you were abducted and forced to live in a foreign land?

_____

_____

_____

_____

_____

_____

_____

2. We can often ignore our own pain when we consider others who we perceive to be worse off – for example, people who have had a traumatic childhood experience. Describe one incident in your past that made you feel disempowered.

_____

_____

_____

_____

_____

_____

_____

3. Do you feel that such an incident or period in your past still has a legacy in your life today?

_____

_____

_____

_____

_____

_____

_____

4. Think of a time when you have made the most of a difficult situation. That could have been in work, at home, school or university for example.

_____

_____

_____

_____

_____

_____

_____

_____

_____

5. Is it easy for you to approach someone in authority? Why or why not?

_____

_____

_____

_____

_____

_____

_____

_____

6. What would be the toughest thing in your life to live without?

_____

_____

_____

_____

_____

_____

_____

_____

Personal Application

It could be said that a large proportion of the Church remains largely unavailable to God due to a disabling submission to circumstances. His desire to use His people is significantly curtailed by a distorted idea that says, 'If only I were free of this, or if only I had the opportunities of brother X – then I'd be a giant for God.'

As we said before, we can easily idealise other people's lives and compare them with our own seemingly dis-advantaged humdrum existence. The great irony of course is that time and again God takes the ordinary, the difficult and, at times, the downright outrageous circumstances of His children and uses them to act as a vehicle for His power.

Seeing Jesus in the Scriptures

Jesus seemed to positively revel in taking a difficult situation and turning it around to His advantage. One can only imagine the pressure He was under as He was constantly chased, questioned and accused. His way of dealing with such pressure was this – He did the things that the Father had set out for Him to do. It's a simple philosophy, but a profoundly effective life motto.

WEEK 6

Leading from the Front

Opening Icebreaker

We've all heard the saying, 'The whole world's a stage.' What movie is playing at your place of work or in your life right now and why?

Bible Readings

• Daniel 6:1–28; 1:1–21

Opening Our Eyes

In our last study we saw that in order for Daniel to be in a position where God could use him, he first had to believe that he could overcome his less than ideal circumstances. It was an important and crucial step, but that was just the beginning.

Daniel 1:8 tells us that 'Daniel resolved not to defile himself'. So not only did Daniel find himself in difficult circumstances, he had made a tough pledge to himself and God to 'keep it pure'. He had been given the opportunity to beef up his team's training schedule with food and wine from the king's table, but Daniel knew this would compromise his faith and tradition.

The next verse in the story is revealing: 'Now God had caused the official to show favour and sympathy to Daniel' (1:9). We are back to the divine blueprint – Daniel plays his part with his decision 'not to defile himself', then the door opens for God to make things happen. Daniel's stance of integrity had become the perfect vehicle for ushering in the divine intervention.

It seems as if Daniel was one of those glass 'half-full' types of people. Whatever the circumstances, he was determined to make the most of them.

As we pick up the story in 1:20 we read: 'In every matter of wisdom and understanding about which the king questioned them, he found them ten times better than all the magicians and enchanters in his whole kingdom.' Once again the stunning combination of God's obedient servant in partnership with his heavenly Father proved irresistible.

Daniel's story goes on to record a miraculous life of huge influence over his contemporaries and even nations – but it all began with his commitment to trust God. And this was with a pagan boss, with occult practitioners as peers and managers! Now, your working environment may be pretty ungodly, but if God can use Daniel in his workplace, there is no reason to doubt that God can do the same in yours.

We have seen how a sense of injustice or a crushing pessimism about our circumstances can have a disabling effect on our effectiveness for God. Daniel was clearly a capable man – but more than that, the Bible tells us he was faithful and honest. His honesty was even evident to those who disliked him, and they claimed that they could find no wrong in him, He went on to serve under three different kings in two different countries – not a bad record for one whose beginnings were so lowly.

Daniel was also much more than a good worker – he was a great leader. Leadership, as those of you who have responsibility in your daily working lives know, is so much more than being in charge. It is a mixture of serving, leading, guiding and standing firm behind the decisions you have made and acting as a living example to your staff. Daniel was a man who exemplified all those qualities, and as we have seen his life was a testimony to the divine blueprint once again making a huge impact on his world and on those around him.

Discussion Starters

1. What current day examples of 'choosing not to defile oneself' can you think of?

_____

_____

_____

_____

_____

_____

_____

_____

2. Would you describe yourself as a glass 'half-empty' or a glass 'half-full' person?

_____

_____

_____

_____

_____

_____

_____

_____

3. How much control over our outlook do you think we have, and can we change such a worldview?

_____

_____

_____

_____

_____

_____

_____

_____

4. Think of examples of good leadership – what were the qualities that made them good?

_____

_____

_____

_____

_____

_____

_____

_____

_____

5. What examples of the flip-side – ie bad examples of leadership – have you experienced, and what impact did they have?

_____

_____

_____

_____

_____

_____

_____

_____

6. If you could have any leadership quality, what would you want?

_____

_____

_____

_____

_____

_____

_____

_____

Personal Application

We can often wonder how on earth God could make an impact in our own day-to-day environment. We may be working under the authority of an unreasonable boss or with blaspheming colleagues. Or it may be that the kind of work we do feels menial or unimportant. Or it is possible that you are out of work and feel even less useful in a society that values employment as a 'badge of respectability'. Whatever the circumstances, if we make a commitment to live out our working lives with integrity, then like Daniel we give God every opportunity to move.

Seeing Jesus in the Scriptures

Some management gurus argue that there is one crucial criterion to measure by when assessing whether or not someone is a leader, and that is – that they have followers. It is easy to stand at the front giving orders and shouting, 'This way everyone', but if you then turn around to find yourself alone, it speaks volumes. Jesus was the supreme leader – He gave direction, He was clear with His message and, most importantly, He led by example. That is why thousands gathered to hear Him speak and others were willing to lay down their lives to follow Him.

WEEK 7

Like Father like Son

Opening Icebreaker

If you were able to perform one miracle right now, what would it be and why?

Bible Readings

- Matthew 13:53–58
- Mark 6:1–6

Opening Our Eyes

' "Where did this man get these things?" they asked. "What's this wisdom that has been given him, that he even does miracles! Isn't this the carpenter?" ' (Mark 6:2–3). It is interesting in this verse, that the one issue that witnesses of the miracles of Jesus couldn't resolve was that He had been a carpenter. Surely, a miracle-maker would have a more prestigious background? Maybe a military training, or priestly qualifications at least? A carpenter?

Carpenters pull on clothes cloudy with wood-dust, nurse blistered hands and stretch weary backs from the long hours. Good carpenters are perfectionists – they have a motto: 'measure twice, cut once'. Skilled carpenters are also problem-solvers, knowing that anything can be fixed. Carpenters are artists, too, understanding that their work can be both functional and beautiful to the eye.

No wonder God chose a carpenter's home in which to place His most beloved Son. Jesus would of course learn the trade of His earthly father. He too would stand over the process of woodcutting, chiselling, hammering and smoothing the rough wood. The hours would have been long, tedious at times, and this gave Him space to consider the relationship between His heavenly mission and the earthly implications (again the Hebrew worldview – no division or contradiction here).

Jesus learned that building and repairing took great strength along with gentleness, persistence with patience, an eye for quality with the appreciation for beauty. He didn't despise such a humble environment, because unlike many in our contemporary culture He didn't make a distinction between the spiritual and the so-called 'natural'. He realised that every act in the earthly realm has a resonance in the heavenlies.

So, as a young man, Jesus finally left His earthly father's carpenter's shop to go into the wider world of humanity. Men and women would now be His craft – many individuals and communities who would recognise the deeper implications of His miracles and profound words. Instinctively they knew that by touching Christ they were touching God. With a heart full of compassion, Jesus the carpenter drew on all His formative experiences and worked at rebuilding and repairing God's creation.

During these studies we have come to see a common thread in the way that God intervenes from His eternal throne into our time–space world – what I have called God's divine blueprint. We have seen that in some ways, reading the headlines of some of the great heroes and heroines of faith can be misleading. It is often in the minor details or domestic elements of the stories that the key to the bigger victories can be found. The life of Christ is no exception.

Have you ever wondered why omnipotent God didn't simply send a 32-year-old Jesus into the world rather than initiate a vastly complicated plan beginning with His miraculous conception in the Virgin Mary. Surely the three 'key years' of Christ's ministry were the real point of God sending His Son? Maybe, but I personally feel it is no coincidence that God chose His way. The divine blueprint would have to be piloted for us by Jesus first – in the day-to-day ups and downs of normal life.

How else could Scripture tell us, 'For we do not have a high priest who is unable to sympathise with our weak-nesses, but we have one who has been tempted in every way, just as we are – yet was without sin' (Heb. 4:15).

The formative years of Jesus' life helped Him connect His earthly ministry with His heavenly destiny – He under-stood and fully engaged in the divine blueprint.

Discussion Starters

1. What are the two best things about your daily routine – in work or in the home etc?

_____

_____

_____

_____

_____

_____

_____

_____

2. Why do you think they are so good – are they related to your 'natural' gifts and personality?

_____

_____

_____

_____

_____

_____

_____

_____

3. What are the worst things about your daily routine – in work or in the home etc?

_____

_____

_____

_____

_____

_____

_____

_____

4. If you had to take something positive from the last answer, what could that be?

_____

_____

_____

_____

_____

_____

_____

_____

_____

5. How do you feel that the divine blueprint could apply to you? Using your creative imagination, paint a picture of a breakthrough that you would love to see in your or another's life.

_____

_____

_____

_____

_____

_____

_____

_____

6. If you could instantly transform one quality of Jesus onto yourself, what would it be?

_____

_____

_____

_____

_____

_____

_____

_____

_____

Personal Application

Many Christians view work as the thing they have to tolerate from Monday to Friday in order to earn money to do God's 'true work' in the evenings and at weekends. You may not identify with that position but here is a question that may reveal your attitude to work and the workplace. Is your expectation to encounter God greater when going to your church meeting or service or when you leave for work on a Monday morning?

Seeing Jesus in the Scriptures

Although we know Jesus as our Saviour and Redeemer, His formative years were spent developing a skill that He was able to translate into a career and in preparation for the great purpose that He came to fulfil. This not only gave Him an insight into the everyday pressures that many of us encounter, but also gave the workplace (whether in the home or the marketplace) a value and status that we devalue at our peril. The blueprint and character for Jesus' ministry was being set down right there in his carpentry apprenticeship and would form valuable lessons and preparation for what was to come.

Leader's Notes

Leader's Notes

Week 1: 'A Woman's Place is ... Doing the Will of God'

Opening Icebreaker

The object of this icebreaker is to quickly get the group to feel connected to each other, which will help with the group dynamics over the coming weeks.

Bible Readings

Generally speaking, the Bible readings throughout these studies are a direct reference to the story being covered. Other supplementary scriptures are there to support as an extra resource. In this first week, Judges describes Deborah's story and John 18:1–11 illustrates the 'Seeing Jesus in the Scriptures' section.

The aim of the suggested Bible readings is to contextualise today's theme with the broader setting of the story of Deborah. It may be useful to have one or two of the group read the scriptures as a foundation for the study session.

Aim of the Session

In this first week it is important that the theme of this study, 'The Divine Blueprint', is established. We live in a church culture that can often polarise the Christian walk into two camps. One is the charismatic superstar preacher who, while brilliantly inspirational, can leave the congregation feeling that superstar leaders will do the important work of God. At the other end of the scale, we see a 'hands-off' leadership style that relies heavily on the church calendar to bring people together, but can seem detached or unrelated to the members' everyday lives. Although this is obviously an over-generalisation, it does show how God's people can become immobilised in their faith walk. We must understand that many of the great works of faith were performed when a fragile human agent joined in partnership with God to stunning effect.

This study is a snapshot of several Old Testament characters with a difference. Instead of focusing on the usual headlines of those stories, it attempts to look behind the scene into the smaller details of their lives and circumstances. The aim is to help believers who perhaps have become so familiar with the stories that they miss the fact that these characters were often ordinary people with one common factor – a simple trust in God. So simple in fact, that despite often difficult circumstances they offered obedience to God who then was able to use them in remarkable ways.

Deborah is a good person to start with. Despite living during such an uncertain time in Israel's history, she was able to remain positive and she acted promptly when required to do so. Her proactive attitude then had impact on those around her, so that God had plenty of willing servants on hand to work with.

It could well be that some of your group have been part of the Church for a long time. They may have heard the great Bible stories, and also the optimistic words of many preachers and fellow-believers – only to feel a sense of let-down in their own lives. Others in the group may be new believers whose understanding of the great Old Testament saints was formed in Sunday School or with bedtime stories. This study aims to point out that it is the ordinary, everyday children of God who can have an impact on their society – if only they trust God and His way of working.

It may be that the Discussion Starters trigger a memory or testimony from one or two of the group. It could be related to them being fearful or living with a sense of disappointment. Don't be afraid to break in and encourage the group to pray for them. It would also be good to follow up that prayer after the session and encourage them to know that God is moving gently, leading them to a secure place. Remember to enquire after them before the next study session.

Hopefully this first session will set the tone for the coming weeks, and create a desire to explore other examples of the divine blueprint in action, of God working in and through His people.

Week 2: To Love and to Obey

Opening Icebreaker

This icebreaker works with groups of any size. It is designed to get the group to open up gently and also to give everyone an opportunity to reveal a little more of themselves.

Once the torch has gone around the circle fully and everyone has shared something, pass it back to a few participants (or everyone if it's a small group) and ask them to expand on what they had shared, eg 'What do you feel are the gaps in your biblical understanding?' or 'Why do you think it's important to have a grasp of Bible teaching?'

Aim of the Session

The theme of this week's study revolves around the familiar story of Jonah. By focusing in on the detail of God's commission to him (to take a message of repentance to Nineveh), we can see Jonah's story is similar to that of so many other saints. It is one thing to claim a faith in Almighty God, it is quite another to live out that faith in obedience to His will.

The discussion should begin to tease out where we each see ourselves in relation to obedience to God. The term 'the fear of God' sounds slightly quaint nowadays, but to earlier generations it had a more significant resonance. It was not so much to be afraid of God Himself, but more a choice of lifestyle that puts obedience to God first – above and beyond any personal priority.

You may want to explore contemporary notions of obedience and authority. It is said that the emerging generation in particular struggle to view authority figures with any credence. Some point to the breakdown of the family and divorce as a cause of this, others to politicians who increasingly stand exposed to accusations of 'sleaze' or unreliability. Whatever the reasoning, it is clear that we live in a time where authority is viewed with suspicion.

This can have a serious impact on our relationship with God. If we struggle with trusting those with power in our everyday lives, then it is not surprising if we have a distorted view of God and His authority.

Jonah almost had to be battered into obeying God, and it could be valuable to look at how taking care to respond in the small issues – one's conscience if you like – is the beginning of a life pleasing to the Father; also, the simplicity of responding to the promptings of the Holy Spirit when reading the Scriptures. These are all simple but effective ways of developing the obedient lifestyle.

You may also need to take care not to inadvertently make the group feel so guilty of their perceived disobedience, that they feel condemned or disqualified. Be attentive to spot the signs of this – members withdrawing from the discussion for example. If Jonah's story tells us anything, it is that God is so gracious that He always leaves the door open to willing repentant souls – whatever their history or background.

Hebrews 12:25–29 is a New Testament command to obey God.

Week 3: Fit for a Queen

Opening Icebreaker
This icebreaker exercise is designed to help people move from a busy mindset filled with the day's issues, and move into study mode. By using the notion of doodling to relax, the group should be able to identify with their own personal visual 'mind mapping' of their day. Mind maps allow us to literally draw a representation of what we view as our imagination or our thinking patterns. Encourage the group to be as open as possible in sharing their perspectives.

Aim of the Session
Esther's world is one that could be seen as far removed from our own experience. The picture seems to portray a culture where women are reduced to commodities, and Esther's life opportunities seem to take a dive when chosen to be part of the king's search for a wife.

It would be easy to say, when viewing Esther's story, that women today have a more quality lifestyle in comparison. While this may be very true, many people still feel that for all the advances made, women still experience issues of prejudice and inequality in our society. It is important to acknowledge such experiences and you could invite female members of the group to share their experiences and perspectives.

Having acknowledged how women face issues even in our culture, it is also crucial to explore how Esther shines as a woman of God who refuses to be overwhelmed in the face of huge disadvantage. This is not just an issue for women, as many saints feel immobilised due to the nature of their circumstances. It is important that the group members know that God understands their feelings and perceptions. It is also critical that believers have the ability to move on from feeling overwhelmed by their circumstances, in order for God to be able to use them.

It is said that one of the problems with the Western world mindset, is that we always compare ourselves with those who have more. We are all touched by materialism in one way or another, but we can make a choice in how we allow this to dictate our lives. Encourage the group to think of situations where people they know are living with a disadvantage greater than their own. It is often when we focus on the needs of others, that we become more able to celebrate the blessings in our own lives – even in the midst of what may be genuinely tough circumstances.

It is also important that the group understand that no circumstances are beyond the reach of God. If we feel that we are without hope, then we become resigned to the status quo. Even a mustard-seed size portion of faith can have a life-changing potential. Encourage the group to explore such miniature faith stepping-stones to a life of overcoming.

Matthew 6:1–8 describes how those with advantaged lifestyles should give with humility.

Week 4: Standing out from the Crowd

Opening Icebreaker

This is meant to be a 'what I need to get the most out of this session' exercise. At the end of this icebreaker you can tell them that their friend, the Holy Spirit is present, and is willing to help them in any way possible.

Aim of the Session

As this is the second part of a study of Esther it would be useful to give an overview of the story so far. It may also be good practice to get the group to review the headlines of some of the spin-off issues raised by part one. Having done this, it should be easy to link the key theme of last week – overcoming our circumstances to serve God effectively – to this week's development of Esther's story.

One of the key things to raise here is that getting our circumstances into perspective is just the beginning. So many people stop at 'first base' and miss the potential blessing as a consequence. It's like the story of the family travelling by car for a picnic. They come to a sign that says 'Beach – 5 miles', stop the car and set up the picnic on the grass below the sign. Sometimes we see the signs of God moving, and mistake that for the actual destination. Esther is a great example of someone fully exploiting the opportunities offered to her – once she had been obedient and had found herself in a position of influence.

One of the key factors to focus upon with Esther's story is once again how explosive the potential of human integrity combined with the power of God can be. Esther displayed courage, honesty, cunning and wisdom in working with the given circumstances. Through no fault of her own, she suddenly had to risk everything in order to save God's people. It would be unlikely that any of the group members have had to go through such an extremely risky situation as Esher's, but they can still identify with her. We have all experienced at some time a feeling of 'no-win' in a situation, and you should attempt to draw real life examples from the group.

It is, however, important that all of us know our own limits and gifting, and have realistic expectations. For example, it may be very straightforward for one person to share his faith to work colleagues. To somebody else, that could feel like a fate worse than death! It isn't necessarily the case that because some are reserved when it comes to witnessing, that they have less faith or are less effective. Living out a life of integrity before our peers can be as effective as a verbal testimony – in some cases more so.

Once again it is crucial to point out the overall theme of the study – the divine blueprint. That when God's saints reach out in their own fragile humanity to the Father, He will always be faithful and join them in an exciting partnership with infinite potential.

Matthew 16:1–12 quotes Jesus in chastising the Pharisees and Sadducees for their wrong motivation in seeking miracles.

Week 5: Stumbling Block or Stepping Stone?

Opening Icebreaker
Our childhood experiences may in fact have left a neg-ative impact on how we respond to change now (children who moved geographic location many times for example), or conversely we can draw upon our historic

child-like innocence and use that as an inspiration to motivate us now.

The icebreaker should lead nicely into the study session and its goal to challenge us all to make the most of our circumstances.

Aim of the Session

For those of us in the west in particular, the impact of growing up in such a culture cannot be overestimated. We are so privileged in so many ways, and we should regularly praise the Lord for our fortunate environment. There are exceptions to this of course, but many of us are highly blessed, but there are some downsides.

A few years ago I took my children on a trip to East Africa to visit some missionary friends. The culture shock was immediate even as we stepped off the plane. Everything from the smells, the temperature and especially the poverty hit us like a stone. It felt like landing on another planet, and took a few days to adjust. It was a life-changing trip for us all, and the new friends we made and the hospitality that we received will stay with us always. There was however one outstanding lesson my children were able to take from the experience. They were able to see first hand that not every child in the world has a Playstation – or their own bedroom, or fresh food everyday, or water from a tap … Also, that for all our material blessing, genuine human values are what count in the end.

The key to this week's session is to challenge the group without condemning them. Sometimes if we over-emphasise the material gap between our culture and that of the emerging nations, we can lose our audience. The skill is to create space for the group to reflect on their circumstances, and see the opportunities that they offer them.

One of the other issues that you should be sensitive to, is if some in your group are living with a real sense of disempowerment in their lives. It may be a broken marriage or bereavement. These feelings may not be related to a geographic foreign land, but nevertheless it can feel daunting – like living in an alien emotional place. If such an intimate sharing should occur, don't rush the study on too quickly – allow space for the individual to share and for the group to gently support.

Week 6: Leading from the Front

Opening Icebreaker
The saying, 'The whole world's a stage' is the kind of statement that if explored offers a whole range of interest-ing opportunities for reflection. Most of us love watching movies and the one thing they all do is invite us to identify with the main character or protagonist.
If the group responses tend to be one-line answers, get them to unpack their choice in more detail: eg, How does it end? What were the obstacles that the character had to overcome? etc.

Aim of the Session
Having seen in our last session how Daniel capitalised on unpromising circumstances, and with a positive attitude made the most of his opportunities, now we see how that was to prove foundational to bringing the divine blueprint into focus. He simply made a decision to keep himself pure. Such a decision should not be underestimated.

To achieve things by 'bending the rules' or 'playing the game', can be very tempting when we find ourselves with a chance of advancing our own cause. Most of us face such a dilemma on a regular basis – maybe even every day. It would be good to get the group to draw a line in the sand when it comes to such a temptation. You could ask for examples of real situations where, for example, a dilemma at work or with a colleague has arisen. Maybe it is to do with seeing something unethical and 'blowing the whistle'. Challenge the group to make a decision as to where their lines are drawn.

In the case of Daniel, the divine blueprint was a three-part situation: he makes the most of very tough circumstances, he makes a decision the 'keep it pure' as a lifestyle, and thirdly, because of his obedience, God steps in to add the divine spark.

It is important that the group feel that they all have the potential to follow Daniel's example. He was free from the Western thirst for material blessing – he simply refused to see his circumstances as overwhelming. He not only made the best of every opportunity that came his way, but also saw his leadership skills emerge and mature. Once given responsibility and power, he never forgot to whom to give the glory – his heavenly Father. As such he was a leader who gained the respect of his peers and his masters – a rare gift indeed.

You may want to tease out where the group feel in relation to the boss–employee relationship. Draw on Daniel's example as a benchmark for how we should approach working relationships.

Week 7: Like Father like Son

Opening Icebreaker
This icebreaker is designed to remind the group that however tough the circumstances of everyday life

become, we are in relationship with the God of miracles – miracles that He is more than capable of performing at any time in any life.

Aim of the Session

During these studies we have taken a 'behind the scenes' approach to some of the great Old Testament heroes and heroines of faith. It seems entirely appropriate to end our exploration with Jesus. Why? Simply because, however useful it is to study those who came before Him in a search for a guide to following God, it is only the Son of God who lived out and perfected the divine blueprint. Everyone else (and we could make the case for many more shining examples) had at least one issue that separates them from Jesus' example – they were all flawed humans. Only Christ perfected what others sought to achieve, and as a result operates as the supreme role-model.

It is not that we now disregard the examples of the past six weeks, far from it. We have seen time and again, how God loves to form a union between the imperfect human agent and His own divine power. It is crucial that in looking at Jesus in this final study, the group hold fast to the truths grasped in discovering the divine blueprint.

It is when looking at Jesus' formative years, however, that we see He did not exclude Himself from the everyday details of life that we all face. A closer look at the early years suggest that this was not simply a growing-up experience – a preamble before the real work of His life mission. It seems that Jesus was taking everything in from a very early age. His daily routine as a carpenter not only gave Him a craft and trade, but a small safe training environment that was preparing Him for everything that was to come.

It is tragic that so many believers view their work or daily routine as a means to an end. I have heard on numerous occasions people say things like, 'I see work as the place I earn money to live – but if only I could serve the Lord full-time ...' I know it's a well-worn cliché now, but we are all full-time for the Lord, and if we could see the potential that we have to transform our world through small victories, then who knows what we could achieve. It's like someone said, 'We can't change everyone's world everywhere, but we can change somebody's world somewhere.'

Challenge the group to see how our everyday life experience offers multiple opportunities to engage with the divine blueprint. A friend of mine has a motto for when he faces challenges – especially intrapersonal difficulties. He says, 'This situation is there to bring out the need in me.' So if an irritating work colleague causes him to become frustrated, he sees it as highlighting a need for him to develop patience or understanding. He's no sinless saint – he does lose it like all of us, but isn't it a great life statement to live by.

End this study by getting the group to headline what they perceive as the 'highlights' of the past few weeks. It will be different for everyone and a time of reflection and prayer will seal revelational truths that will hopefully live with them in the coming weeks and years.

NATIONAL DISTRIBUTORS

UK: (and countries not listed below)
CWR, Waverley Abbey House, Waverley Lane, Farnham, Surrey GU9 8EP.
Tel: (01252) 784700 Outside UK (44) 1252 784700 Email: mail@cwr.org.uk

AUSTRALIA: KI Entertainment, Unit 21 317-321 Woodpark Road, Smithfield,
New South Wales 2164.
Tel: 1 800 850 777 Fax: 02 9604 3699 Email: sales@kientertainment.com.au

CANADA: David C Cook Distribution Canada, PO Box 98, 55 Woodslee Avenue,
Paris, Ontario N3L 3E5.
Tel: 1800 263 2664 Email: swansons@cook.ca

GHANA: Challenge Enterprises of Ghana, PO Box 5723, Accra.
Tel: (021) 222437/223249 Fax: (021) 226227 Email: ceg@africaonline.com.gh

HONG KONG: Cross Communications Ltd, 1/F, 562A Nathan Road, Kowloon.
Tel: 2780 1188 Fax: 2770 6229 Email: cross@crosshk.com

INDIA: Crystal Communications, 10-3-18/4/1, East Marredpalli, Secunderabad
– 500026, Andhra Pradesh.
Tel/Fax: (040) 27737145 Email: crystal_edwj@rediffmail.com

KENYA: Keswick Books and Gifts Ltd, PO Box 10242-00400, Nairobi.
Tel: (254) 20 312639/3870125 Email: keswick@swiftkenya.com

MALAYSIA: Salvation Book Centre (M) Sdn Bhd, 23 Jalan SS 2/64,
47300 Petaling Jaya, Selangor.
Tel: (03) 78766411/78766797 Fax: (03) 78757066/78756360
Email: info@salvationbookcentre.com

Canaanland, No. 25 Jalan PJU 1A/41B, NZX Commercial Centre, Ara Jaya,
47301 Petaling Jaya, Selangor.
Tel: (03) 7885 0540/1/2 Fax: (03) 7885 0545 Email: info@canaanland.com.my

NEW ZEALAND: KI Entertainment, Unit 21 317-321 Woodpark Road, Smithfield,
New South Wales 2164, Australia.
Tel: 0 800 850 777 Fax: +612 9604 3699 Email: sales@kientertainment.com.au

NIGERIA: FBFM, Helen Baugh House, 96 St Finbarr's College Road, Akoka, Lagos.
Tel: (01) 7747429/4700218/825775/827264 Email: fbfm@hyperia.com

PHILIPPINES: OMF Literature Inc, 776 Boni Avenue, Mandaluyong City.
Tel: (02) 531 2183 Fax: (02) 531 1960 Email: gloadlaon@omflit.com

SINGAPORE: Alby Commercial Enterprises Pte Ltd, 95 Kallang Avenue #04-00,
AIS Industrial Building, 339420.
Tel: (65) 629 27238 Fax: (65) 629 27235 Email: marketing@alby.com.sg

SOUTH AFRICA: Struik Christian Books, 80 MacKenzie Street, PO Box 1144,
Cape Town 8000.
Tel: (021) 462 4360 Fax: (021) 461 3612 Email: info@struikchristianmedia.co.za

SRI LANKA: Christombu Publications (Pvt) Ltd, Bartleet House, 65 Braybrooke
Place, Colombo 2.
Tel: (9411) 2421073/2447665 Email: dhanad@bartleet.com

USA: David C Cook Distribution Canada, PO Box 98, 55 Woodslee Avenue, Paris,
Ontario N3L 3E5, Canada. Tel: 1800 263 2664 Email: swansons@cook.ca

CWR is a Registered Charity - Number 294387
CWR is a Limited Company registered in England -
Registration Number 1990308

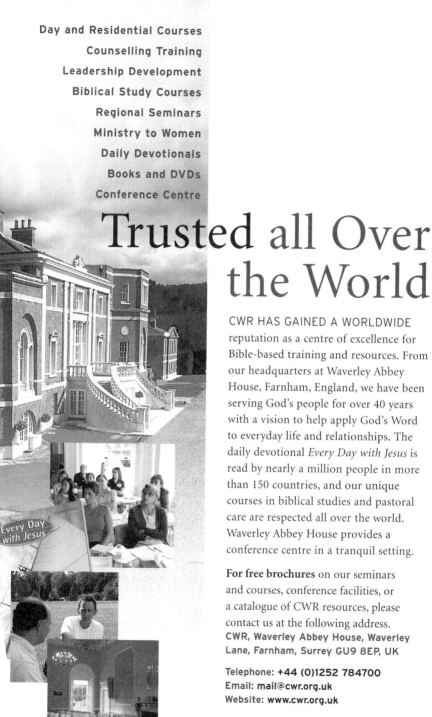

Day and Residential Courses

Counselling Training

Leadership Development

Biblical Study Courses

Regional Seminars

Ministry to Women

Daily Devotionals

Books and DVDs

Conference Centre

Trusted all Over the World

CWR HAS GAINED A WORLDWIDE reputation as a centre of excellence for Bible-based training and resources. From our headquarters at Waverley Abbey House, Farnham, England, we have been serving God's people for over 40 years with a vision to help apply God's Word to everyday life and relationships. The daily devotional *Every Day with Jesus* is read by nearly a million people in more than 150 countries, and our unique courses in biblical studies and pastoral care are respected all over the world. Waverley Abbey House provides a conference centre in a tranquil setting.

For free brochures on our seminars and courses, conference facilities, or a catalogue of CWR resources, please contact us at the following address. **CWR, Waverley Abbey House, Waverley Lane, Farnham, Surrey GU9 8EP, UK**

Telephone: **+44 (0)1252 784700**
Email: mail@cwr.org.uk
Website: www.cwr.org.uk

CWR Applying God's Word
to everyday life and relationships

Dramatic new resources

2 Corinthians: Restoring harmony
by Christine Platt

Paul's message went against the grain of the culture in Corinth, and even his humility was in stark contrast to Greco–Roman culture. Be challenged and inspired to endure suffering, seek reconciliation, pursue holiness and much more as you look at this moving letter which reveals Paul's heart as much as his doctrine. This thought-provoking, seven-week study guide is great for individual or small-group use.
ISBN: 978-1-85345-551-3

Isaiah 40–66: Prophet of restoration
by John Houghton

God is a God of new beginnings, a God of second chances who takes no pleasure in punishment. However, profound lessons must be learned if the same errors are to be avoided in the future. Understand Isaiah's powerful message for each of us, that God is a holy God who cannot ignore sin, but One who also displays amazing grace and mercy, and who longs to enjoy restored relationship with us. These seven inspiring and challenging studies are perfect for individual or small-group use.
ISBN: 978-1-85345-550-6

Also available in the bestselling
Cover to Cover Bible Study Series

1 Corinthians
Growing a Spirit-filled church
ISBN: 978-1-85345-374-8

2 Corinthians
Restoring harmony
ISBN: 978-1-85345-551-3

1 Timothy
Healthy churches – effective Christians
ISBN: 978-1-85345-291-8

23rd Psalm
The Lord is my shepherd
ISBN: 978-1-85345-449-3

2 Timothy and Titus
Vital Christianity
ISBN: 978-1-85345-338-0

Ecclesiastes
Hard questions and spiritual answers
ISBN: 978-1-85345-371-7

Ephesians
Claiming your inheritance
ISBN: 978-1-85345-229-1

Esther
For such a time as this
ISBN: 978-1-85345-511-7

Fruit of the Spirit
Growing more like Jesus
ISBN: 978-1-85345-375-5

Genesis 1–11
Foundations of reality
ISBN: 978-1-85345-404-2

God's Rescue Plan
Finding God's fingerprints on human histo
ISBN: 978-1-85345-294-9

Great Prayers of the Bible
Applying them to our lives today
ISBN: 978-1-85345-253-6

Hebrews
Jesus – simply the best
ISBN: 978-1-85345-337-3

Hosea
The love that never fails
ISBN: 978-1-85345-290-1

£3.99 each (plus p&p)
Price correct at time of printing

Cover to Cover Every Day
Gain deeper knowledge of the Bible

Each issue of these bimonthly daily Bible-reading notes gives you insightful commentary on a book of the Old and New Testaments with reflections on a Psalm each weekend by Philip Greenslade.

Enjoy contributions from two well-known authors every two months, and over a five-year period you will be taken through the entire Bible.

ISSN: 1744-0114
Only £2.49 each (plus p&p)
£13.80 for annual UK subscription (6 issues)
£13.80 for annual email subscription
(available from www.cwr.org.uk/store)

Cover to Cover Complete
Read through the Bible chronologically

Take an exciting, year-long journey through the Bible, following
events as they happened.

- See God's strategic plan of redemption unfold across the
  centuries
- Increase your confidence in the Bible as God's inspired message
- Come to know your heavenly Father in a deeper way

The full text of the flowing Holman Christian Standard Bible
(HCSB) provides an exhilarating reading experience and is
augmented by our beautiful:

- Illustrations
- Maps
- Charts
- Diagrams
- Timeline

And key Scripture verses
and devotional thoughts
make each day's reading
more meaningful.

ISBN: 978-1-85345-433-2
Only £19.99 (plus p&p)

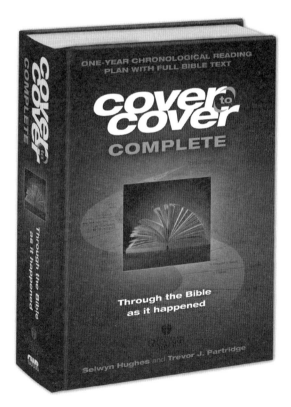